Awaken your Gratitude

Ignite your positivity in 14 days!

Lillian Carlyle

direct or indirect, that are incurred as a result of the use of the information contained within this document, including, but not limited to, errors, omissions, or inaccuracies.

Table of Contents

Introduction

A grateful mind is a great mind which eventually attracts to itself great things. –Plato

We can all resonate with those moments when it feels like the world has entirely engulfed us, right? You know, those times when we decide to play hide-and-seek, burrowing under the covers of our trusty bed fortresses, leaving only a strategic peephole for the eyes? Well, that's not exactly the best logical move. It's a common feeling; however, it raises an important question: How do we lift our spirits during these seemingly delicate moments?

I have one word for you: gratitude. Now, I can almost hear those questions buzzing in your head. *Where can I find the time to do this? Can I even afford this? How long will it take to master?*

The attitude of gratitude is not a complex skill that demands an elaborate production. It also doesn't demand much time or cost a dime. There's a myriad of possibilities to incorporate gratitude into our lives. Some prefer journaling; others some vibrant colors and a canvas. Yet, a good dose of awareness about the positive aspects swirling around us and a simple "thank you" sprinkled throughout the day will also suffice. According to positive psychology research, gratitude is the golden ticket to experiencing higher levels of happiness *Gratitude: Fun Facts and App Recommendations*, n.d.)! It opens the floodgates to an onslaught of positive emotions, fantastical experiences, improved health, and more meaningful relationships.

Remember, as a child, when joy and fulfillment were as accessible as candy from a candy store? Do you recall the boundless optimism, especially during holidays and birthdays? There was an abundance of laughter and playfulness, with mismatched socks and spilled milk, almost as if it flowed so effortlessly with no towering to-do lists and buried responsibilities consuming much of the day. These exact same occurrences now spark frustration in adulthood, starkly contrasting the carefree joy and smiles of childhood. Well, these towering to-do lists are inevitable in adulthood, but the challenge lies in not allowing them to overwhelm us and cause us to neglect the little moments of positivity around us. That enthusiasm still resides within us; we all have the capacity to greet each day with a mind brimming with curiosity—a mind that is grateful and eager.

It's time to push that rewind button to reacquaint ourselves with joy and learn how to live in the present again, relishing the positivity that surrounds us. Every little aspect or moment counts, accumulating and collectively turning our days into fulfilling tapestries. And, how exactly do we set forth on this gratitude journey?

You're in the right place at the right time. This book serves as your roadmap back to that pure, unadulterated joy. It will guide you to revel in the present and bask in its sheer delight, instead of fixating on the "could haves" and "should haves." You see, it's a conscious decision we make. We have the freedom to choose what we focus on. And, let's not forget: Energy flows where attention goes. When we opt to focus on what's absent, it's a guarantee that our emotional tide will ebb to the shores of negativity. But direct your focus to the goodness that graces you, and you are fueling the fires of positivity. The alchemy of gratitude is a journey comprised of baby steps. After all, Rome didn't sprout forth in a single sunrise. Cultivating the attitude of gratitude as a steadfast companion in your life requires some solid determination and a patient hand.

I have written this book to help you do just that, pacing us evenly through one chapter at a time. And don't fret You can take it at your own pace, ensuring each step leaves a lasting footprint. However, no shortcuts are possible, and there are no quick fixes here; consistency is key. It's time to embrace a new routine that starts and wraps up each day with gratitude, as well as sprinkling some of that goodness throughout the hours. And here's a little secret before we get started: It helps to throw a smile into the mix. It amplifies the power of positivity, triggering a ripple effect of love, and it even comes with a whole list of added bonuses, such as stress relief. And the best part? It won't cost you a dime; smiling is absolutely free!

As a matter of fact, why not give it a whirl right now? Even if it might feel a tad odd, put a smile on that dial of yours, and tap into this magnificent wellspring of contentment. It's a complete game-changer. I guarantee this!

Without further ado, let's delve into the art of cultivating gratitude!

Chapter 1:

The Art of Gratitude

*Do not spoil what you have by desiring what you have not; remember
that what you now have was once among the things you only hoped for.*
–Epicurus

The ancient concept of gratitude is tightly woven into the
fabric of our existence. This profound practice—resilient
against the sands of time and borders of culture—has
found resonance in philosophy, culture, and religion.

The ancient Greek philosopher Epicurus grasped this secret
well. He saw gratitude as the very cornerstone of a life well-
lived, and his teachings echo, reminding us to relish in life's

simpler joys. Another great thinker in this area was the Roman polymath Cicero, who deemed gratitude to be a moral compass guiding human interaction. But the story of gratitude doesn't end here. Around the globe, various cultural practices and religious scriptures herald gratitude as a transcendent force. From Eastern philosophies right through to Zen practice, all teach the same timeless truth: Acknowledging the gifts of life is the ultimate path to inner peace and enlightenment.

But what exactly makes gratitude such a powerful force with regard to the human experience?

Simply put, gratitude is an art form that entails consciously acknowledging the positive aspects of our lives. Irrespective of how big or small they are, we have to actively appreciate and celebrate them. It's a true transformative power that can alter our perception of the world, shifting it from lack to abundance.

And no, it's not mere folklore. Gratitude is recognized as having significant positive impacts on psychological and physical health, improving overall well-being and quality of life. It triggers the release of happy hormones, such as serotonin and dopamine, enhancing mood, improving sleep, fortifying our immune systems, and giving stress a good run for its money. The attitude of gratitude shifts our perspectives to better navigate challenges with greater resilience. It allows us to express appreciation and cultivate a sense of belonging. It creates a chain reaction of goodwill and kindness, fostering deeper connections with others and the world around us.

Furthermore, we find ourselves in a society that is haunted by the pursuit of more, more, and more. Gratitude is that beacon of light, reminding us to pause and enjoy what we do have, allowing us to bask in the richness of our own existence. Gratitude is the key that unlocks a fresh, abundant mindset, replacing scarcity with a realization of the blessings that often go unnoticed in our surroundings. It highlights that we already have all we truly need to live a happy life.

The practice of gratitude has withstood the test of time across different cultures and philosophies. It's more than a fleeting emotion; it's the gateway to fulfillment, and it is most certainly an art worth cultivating in our lives.

Chapter 2:

Day 1—Make a List

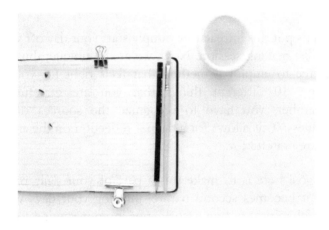

Be thankful for everything that happens in your life; it's all an experience. –Roy T. Bennett

Oh yes, this is day one, and it's time to get creative! We shall keep it short and sweet. And that in itself is already something to be grateful for among the myriad of other things in your life.

Research has a nifty way of putting it: Gratitude is both a state and a trait (Jans-Beken et al., 2019). This is a profoundly powerful realization because it means that we are not only capable of experiencing gratitude for a certain moment in time, but we can also adopt it as a positive, more permanent character trait. Dr. Robert Emmons further sets it out, saying gratitude involves recognizing the good things in your life and appreciating where they come from (Emmons & McCullough, 2003).

Exercise

So, let's put this into action. Simply start your day off with a little list-making session. Now, we are all unique; thus, you are free to employ a method that feels right for you and present 10 different things that you are grateful for. Remember, you have to recognize the sources of this goodness. This allows for a deeper reflection on the aspects you are grateful for.

The goal here is to make this a part of your daily routine until it becomes second nature, infusing your days with a grateful spirit. So, find a cozy spot in your routine to fit it in, just like we discussed. As you keep at it, you'll start noticing even more things to be grateful for every single day.

Let's look at some examples to get the ball on the roll:

- an invigorating hot shower that allows you a fresh start to each day

- your perfect morning brew that kickstarts your day

- your wonderful spouse who adds immense joy and value to your life.

- those precious, quiet moments that grant you time for reflection

- the ability to move and exercise that keeps your body in optimal physical condition

- every bite of food you take that nourishes your body

- the serene sounds of nature, like rustling leaves and chirping birds, that provide a tranquil backdrop

- the people who are true treasures who make you laugh and smile

- the roof over your head that provides comfort, warmth, and a sense of security

- your job that enables you to generate income, supporting both yourself and others

- yes, even that old alarm clock, faithfully ensuring that you're always on time

Strategies

- It's not just about stating gratitude it's about recognizing and comprehending the reasons behind each thing you are grateful for. You need to fully immerse yourself in each sentiment and sentence.

- Take a moment to completely engross yourself in the feeling of gratitude for each component on your list.

- Experience the joy, and be sure to smile. Engage all your senses; smell the flowers, and fully involve yourself in every aspect of the positive emotions you're experiencing.

- Think of the day ahead from a perspective of gratitude. Picture everything aligning to serve you the best way it can. The heavy traffic is inconsequential; you will still reach your destination. Your meeting goes smoothly, your studies and workout sessions are productive, and your meals are delectable. You're going to have a really great day! It doesn't matter what it is, pay that gratitude forward to as many aspects of your day as possible.

- Pay attention to the little things we often take for granted to get a newfound vitality through your appreciation.

- Remember to smile, smile, smile!

Now, as you compile your gratitude list, you are empowering your memory and enriching your life. Jotting down the aspects that you hold near and dear externalizes and solidifies your sentiments. It transcends fleeting thoughts. It takes them from the recesses of your mind and transforms them into tangible, more comprehensible realities. It's like eating a lovely spread of tapas, small and digestible, allowing you to internalize the information with ease. Moreover, your simple list is a catalyst for transformation, forming more enduring habits. It is a vivid reminder of the abundance that surrounds you every day, encouraging you to navigate your precious time with a spirit of wonder and appreciation.

Thus, let that pen dance!

Chapter 3:

Day 2—A Focus Item to Prompt Your Gratitude Each Day

Gratitude turns what we have into enough. –Unknown

Remember, energy flows where focus goes! So, today we are elevating our gratitude practice by embarking on a journey of heightened mindfulness. We are going to hone in on a carefully chosen element that will act as a steadfast trigger, encouraging you to not only express your gratitude but also fully immerse yourself in its embrace.

This is all about taking a pause from life's ceaseless whirlwind and deliberately stepping away from the relentless demands and pressing concerns. This chosen element will be like a key that unlocks your own personal sanctuary of introspection where you can find a moment for appreciation. This tiny moment you grant yourself—this window of time where you step into your own personal sanctuary—will unveil the true weight and significance of the joy that envelops you.

This is a deliberate move toward acknowledging the depth of your experiences that will rekindle the flame of gratitude within you.

Exercise

So, let's kick things off just like before, on Day 1 List another 10 things you are grateful for, expanding your inventory of positivity. Remember, it's all about establishing gratitude as a routine. And you know, in order for it to take root and flourish, you will have to keep it up, be consistent, and regularly nurture the practice.

The added extra for the gratitude practice will require you to pick a focus item! Select an item that resonates with your unique sensibilities. Think of it as a tailor-made approach that will maximize your benefits. It could be a constellation of sticky notes strategically placed throughout your home or a cherished object on your bedside table, offering the gentle nudge to embrace gratitude at the start of your day and as you bid it farewell at night. Alternatively, you can harness the power of technology, setting reminders that will strategically prompt your mindful moments of gratitude.

Let's take a closer look at some great sentence starters:

- Thank you to...

- Thank you for...

- I am so grateful for...

- I am so happy that...

- I'm overjoyed to have...

- It means a lot to me that...

Strategies

- Get emotional and descriptive: As mentioned previously you need to dive in with your heart and soul to the very moment and fully unleash the extraordinary power of gratitude. Don't just be thankful for the flowers, be thankful for the beautiful, vibrant, fragrant flowers that bring you sweet joy! Be grateful for every deep, life-giving breath that fuels your body, keeping your loving heart beautifully breathing to the tender rhythm of life. You are the artist of your gratitude palette, crafting your day with unparalleled beauty. Allow those vibrant descriptions to freely flow, elevating your feel-good vibrations and securing them with that extra layer of positivity.

- Recognize value: Take a moment to truly grasp the profound significance each aspect brings to your life. The things we are grateful for, big or small, elevate our existence in a variety of meaningful ways. Some grant us life itself—consider the breath that sustains you. Your cherished connections provide you with a deep sense of purpose and belonging. Your career offers opportunity. There's so much richness in every layer of our lives—a beautiful, meaningful poetic undercurrent.

- Radiate and smile: That very important smile that accompanies your expression of gratitude? Well, it's also a warm nod to the world for all that's great and wonderful. This smile is a testament that gratitude isn't confined to one fleeting moment. Gratitude is a lifestyle. And, what finer way to navigate life's twists and turns than with a radiant smile illuminating your way? Smile, smile, smile!

One of the biggest reasons we fall short with a lot of the things we set out to do is because we simply forget. We are not reminded. You know how quickly time can slip by us, magically engulfing us in its current. However, reminders have benefits beyond mere recollection. Engaging in the "reminder practice," enables you to be more committed, responsible, focused, and motivated. It allows you to hone self-discipline, and in doing so, it fosters and improves both self-esteem and self-confidence. You are essentially reaping more than a double harvest from the seeds of gratitude!

Now, remember, the best reminder is something that is obvious, easily noticeable, and specific. Here's a splendid reminder: smile, smile, and smile.

Chapter 4:

Day 3—End Your Day With

Gratitude

When I started counting my blessings, my whole life turned around. –
Willie Nelson

You guessed it! Add another 10 gems to your list of things to be grateful for, even if they overlap with some of your previous entries. It's all about maintaining that consistent flow.

Journey along throughout your day, filled with your focus items and reminders. These beacons are your reminder to pause, take a breath, and be grateful. These little intervals should never be underestimated; see them as continuous little investments you make in your overall well-being.

So, you have started your day with gratitude; you have it sprinkled throughout the day. But there's one more crucial aspect to this story: the closing act, if you will. This is a moment you take to reflect back on the day and pay attention to all the beautiful moments that contributed to your joy. Thus, today's bonus task is to rewind your day in your mind's eye, going back to its inception, reflecting on your experiences, and recognizing all the reasons you have for gratitude before you get some shut-eye.

Yet again, this is a tailor-made experience. Whether it's done during your relaxing evening stroll, while you brush your teeth, or as you slip into your comfy pajamas, it's all good. As long as it resonates with you and forms part of your bedtime routine, marking the grand exit of your day.

Exercise

What is it that makes life truly enchanting? The fact that every day unfolds its own unique story!

Yes, some days are a bit of a wild ride, leaving us feeling a bit flustered and rough around the edges. But it's especially during these moments that we need to reflect and acknowledge the essence of life's beauty. With gratitude, you can truly turn lemons into lemonade. You will notice when you take time out to reflect on all the significant moments that unfolded throughout the day, that not one single day in our lives lacks its own essence of gratitude. Size doesn't diminish the impact of positivity. Whether small or grand, these moments stitch the day together, helping us pull through. It's the silent fuel that propels us forward.

Let's look at a few examples of what you can cherish and reflect upon at the closing of each day's special chapter:

- I'm thankful for that heartwarming phone call from my friend, mother, or brother—it was a moment that provided me with a sense of belonging.

- How amazing was that walk through the park during my lunch break? I could get in touch with nature, appreciate its beauty, and experience a sense of groundedness.

- I am so pleased that my meeting ran smoothly and for the support and appreciation from my coworkers who filled the room with such positive energy.

- It was a true blessing to be able to sit around the dinner table with my family and experience each one of them radiating their own unique light.

- I am grateful for the commute to and from work that gifted me with a chance to witness the world around me, reminding me of how vast and beautiful life can be.

- A special thanks to the cashier at my local grocery store. Their assistance made it possible for me to purchase what I needed.

- Reflecting on it all, I'm grateful for every single good thing that unfolded today.

Strategies

- Reflect on the highlights: Start by recalling all the positive moments from your day. This could range from a successful task right through to a simple, kind gesture.

- Visualize: Close your eyes, and revisit each moment, allowing yourself to relive the associated emotions. This will further reinforce a strong sensation of gratitude.

- Set intentions for the next day: Express gratitude for the day ahead by setting positive intentions. This is an excellent way to start the day with positivity and a clear sense of purpose.

Yet again, weaving gratitude into your bedtime routine isn't just about drifting off with a more positive outlook, it also enhances the quality of your sleep. You can look forward to fewer sleep disturbances, providing your body with the uninterrupted time it needs for restorative processes. This all ensures you wake up feeling in tip-top shape, ready to seize each new day with full vigor.

For a peaceful slumber and a fresh start come morning, remember that radiant smile as you conclude your day with gratitude!

Chapter 5:

Day 4—Family

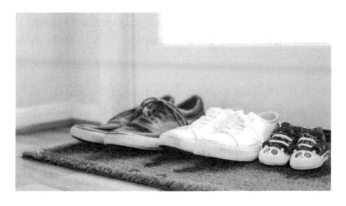

The more grateful I am, the more beauty I see. –Mary Davis

We have successfully completed three days of consciously honing in on gratitude! Bravo! This is only the starting point, though; there is still so much to look forward to when the attitude of gratitude takes root! Let's continue nurturing this incredible superpower.

Keep up the momentum, adding those 10 additional gratitude gems to your list, taking those little self-reflection moments throughout the day, and closing off the day with your heart brimming with gratitude.

Today, it's all about family. Oh yes! They come in all shapes and sizes, but whether big or small, a family filled with love is a true gift. I call it a true gift because the unfortunate reality is that not everyone is blessed with a complete, joy-filled, supportive family. Thus, never underestimate the miracle of yours. Likewise, aim to never compare yours; they are all unique. Family is more than just faces around the dinner table. They offer a sense of belonging, security, profound purpose, and most importantly, boundless love. Look at the cherished lifetime of memories you create with each member that forms part of this precious unit, along with the guidance, encouragement, and stability they provide.

Now, how do you express love towards your family? The simple answer: in a myriad of ways! One of those includes being grateful for each member who forms part of this integral unit.

Exercise

Take a quiet moment, and reflect on your family. Select three family members, and identify five reasons why you are grateful for each of them. You can pen these down in a journal or simply contemplate them in your mind. Remember to use your imagination and get vivid with those descriptions.

Now, we can all most certainly resonate with the whirlwind of a vibrant family life. This includes those frustrating moments, the uncertainties, and all the riveting rollercoaster rides composed of ups and downs. This is rather standard, all forming part of the journey. Amidst those twists and turns, there is always something to be grateful for, and your task is to extract gratitude and love from any given situation. There is no hard and fast rule when it comes to gratitude; remember, it knows no bounds. Perhaps, you hold your friends very close and dear, considering them part of your family or vice versa. It doesn't matter if there is a "blood" connection, count them all to recognize the abundance of blessings you have to be grateful for when it comes to family.

Let's pause for a moment and look at some of the people and scenarios you might consider to kick-start gratitude when it comes to your family:

- a sister who always lends a helping hand with the kids

- a brother who's always there to serve as your trusted confidant

- a father who patiently taught you how to drive, ride a bike, or play a round of golf

- a child who showers you with affectionate kisses and warm hugs

- those large, rowdy, noisy, fun family gatherings

- the intimate, more quiet gatherings of just a select few

- the grandchildren that bring endless joy, laughter, and love into your life

- even if they are few and far between, the cherished moments and phone conversations spent with an elderly parent or grandparent

- that irksome family member—summon your best effort to find something to be grateful for in them as well

When it comes to appreciating and feeling grateful for the people in our lives, physically expressing that gratitude not only makes you feel more grateful but also cultivates it as a lasting state. Now, let's step into some strategies that will help up the gratitude game.

Strategies

- Focus on the positive: Focus on one positive aspect of your family member. It could be a character trait, a fond memory, or a moment you shared. When you focus on these positives, you naturally cultivate a more positive perception of them.

- Promote honesty and sincerity: Being truly grateful for someone requires both honesty and sincerity. Honesty is required to truly experience the fulfillment of gratitude, and sincerity, on the other hand, adds true intention to your experience. If, for instance, you've included that irksome family member on your list, you can be honest about their flaws, yet approach them with sincerity and compassion to uncover that one thing you're grateful for about them.

- Promote gratitude: As important as it is to experience gratitude, promoting gratitude within your family is just as important. There are plenty of things you can do to spread the love and power of gratitude. It's contagious!

  o Have each person say one nice thing about the person to their right during dinner or breakfast.

  o Write a short and sweet note to a family member expressing why and how much you appreciate them.

  o Verbally express thankfulness to your family members.

  o Give compliments.

  o Give plenty of hugs and affection.

  o Regularly offer a helping hand.

  o Spend more time together, playing games, doing chores, or cooking meals.

  o Practice more patience.

Having the art of gratitude form a fundamental cornerstone in your family lays a strong foundation for other relationships, enabling every person to form more secure, healthy attachments. This fosters an environment where individuals feel genuinely cared for and safe, subsequently leading to enhanced social functioning.

As you can see, gratitude is the gift that keeps on giving and most certainly a seed well worth planting in the heart of any home! Remember to keep smiling!

Chapter 6:

Day 5—Relationships

Let us be grateful to people who make us happy, they are the charming gardeners who make our souls blossom. —Marcel Proust

Continue with your list, expanding with 10 additional gratitude gems; pause throughout the day, and feel grateful for the beauty and blessings that envelop you. Last, but most certainly not least, remember to end your day with gratitude.

Our special added extra for Day 5 is all about healing and finding peace. Peaceful people are powerful people with hearts that harbor great strength. It's in moments of tranquility that our minds find some peace amidst the chaos of life. This step is designed to help you reclaim that power. The power of forgiveness has a great influence on cultivating inner peace, leading to a more fulfilled balanced life. When your mind is at peace and your heart is filled with forgiveness, you navigate life with more grace, resilience, wisdom, and clarity. The best part about this? You are unburdened by resentments and grudges, liberated from the shackles of past grievances! This is a very powerful way to lighten your load on this journey called life. Think of it as an antidote to stress and anxiety that take a significant toll on your emotional and physical well-being. It's your shield against negativity, offering you a brighter, more positive outlook on life.

And don't overlook the significant emotional impact it holds, fostering greater empathy and deeper connections with others. Forgiveness and mental peace also liberate your imagination from fear of the unknown, unleashing your creativity. It allows you to boldly step forth, embracing new ideas, approaches, and experiences.

Cultivated through self-reflection, mindfulness, and the practice of gratitude, inner peace serves as your gateway to a more harmonious life.

Exercise

Pick one person or relationship that could use some improvement. Take a moment to assess the situation and find 10 aspects of relationships that you are grateful for, even amid the difficulties. This is certainly easier said than done, but trust me, the sense of liberation is well worth the time and effort.

When we hold onto bitterness and harbor resentment, it's hard to forgive, let alone find things to be grateful for. Remember, this is about you; it's all about your healing and release of resentment, ultimately leading to greater happiness and contentment in your life. It doesn't mean that you have to condone the harmful actions of others, nor does it necessitate you to interact with them. This process is not about them; it's about taking back your power and not allowing external influences to hinder your fulfillment. Through the practice of gratitude, you have the strength to navigate this path toward personal empowerment and inner peace:

- You may not always see eye-to-eye with your partner, but perhaps, they offer invaluable support, lightening the load of everyday responsibilities and assisting with childcare and chores. It's important to recognize and hone in on the positive qualities.

- Friendships are as diverse as the people who form them. Some friends are constant presences in our daily lives, offering a stronger sense of reliability. Others may be more distant, but they still provide meaning, whether it be a couple of sporadic catch-up conversations or a planned annual meet-up. Embrace and be grateful for the uniqueness of each friendship.

- If you're harboring bitterness towards an ex-partner, remember there was once something that drew you to them in the first place. There was something you once admired enough to embark on a journey with them. There are even lessons you have learned about yourself from your time together. Even a tiny glimpse of gratitude towards them can cast a light on the shadows, paving the way for greater happiness.

- Perhaps, you're estranged from a family member or dear friend. Identify three things you're grateful to them for. Maybe, they were your best playmate at school. Perhaps, they helped you land your first job. You don't have to take immediate action to mend the relationship; you don't even have to take any physical action at all. It's all dependent on your individual situation. However, cultivating gratitude for these small gestures can significantly diminish anger and resentment towards them. Healing takes time, but every step you take towards it is a step in the right direction.

Strategies

- It's about you: First and foremost, forgiveness is about you and honoring your needs. It is a step you take towards finding your own inner peace. You must understand that forgiveness is an internal process—a journey primarily for you.

- Gain some perspective: Practicing forgiveness is not a walk in the park; it can be rather painful working through those complex emotions. Take a step back and view the situation from an objective standpoint.

You'll notice that often, those who cause pain are grappling with their own pain and inner struggles.

- Let it go: We don't always have all the answers in life. A lot of the time, we might not comprehend the actions of another. Yet again, shift your perspective from anger and pain to the choice of letting go and liberating yourself.

- Talk about it: Put your feelings into words, articulating and labeling them. This will require you to recognize and accept your emotions, even the unpleasant ones. Identifying these emotions makes it easier for you to pinpoint what exactly it is that needs to be released within yourself. You can't keep it confined within the recesses of your mind; you need to let it out. You are not responsible for the actions of another; however, your power resides within how you choose to respond to a given situation. You can write it down, say it out loud to yourself, or speak to a trusted person about it, as long as you express it.

- Recognize what you've gained: In general, when emotions run high, it's hard to see the blessings or the lessons that may emerge. Grant yourself some patience, space, and time to gain a fresh perspective. Maybe, a friend let you down and did something hurtful. Despite your animosity and pain, grant yourself some time to delve deeper for a better understanding. Perhaps, it was related to their mental health. Armed with this newfound clarity, you will now be in a position where you can extend much-needed support to both yourself and your friend.

- Start small: It's normal to find it challenging to forgive. However, start small. Begin with yourself; practice self-compassion, and forgive any initial self-blame. This will help you get more accustomed to the act of forgiveness, encouraging you to forgive more regularly. Remember, charity starts at home, and extending compassion and forgiveness to yourself sets the foundation for forgiving others.

Practicing gratitude is the key to unlocking a fulfilling, nurturing path for your personal growth, along with a good dose of self-compassion and kindness. The more you nurture yourself, the more you have to give to others. Embrace every aspect of yourself, imperfections and all This will enable you to better understand, forgive, and embrace others.

And be sure to put a good dose of intention behind every action, along with that ever-important smile!

Chapter 7:

Day 6—Health and Body

Let us rise up and be thankful, for if we didn't learn a lot at least we learned a little, and if we didn't learn a little, at least we didn't get sick, and if we got sick, at least we didn't die; so, let us all be thankful. –Buddha

Start off Day 7 just as every other day: Expand your list, take moments to recognize the abundance surrounding you, and express gratitude; then, end your day with gratitude.

For today, you will be required to list 10 things about your health or body that you are grateful for. One of the biggest things that we often easily overlook is to be grateful for this incredible gift. We tend to take it for granted as if it's a given. When was the last time you took a moment to pause and truly appreciate your amazing body? Personally, I've spent years being extremely critical of my reflection. All I saw was "too heavy," "too short," "not tanned enough"—I have been there. Recently, however, I started being more content with my reflection. I truly started appreciating what I saw, all thanks to the practice of gratitude.

Our bodies are a true marvel to behold, deserving of our appreciation and gratitude. Most of us are lucky enough to have legs that faithfully carry us where we need to go; hands that allow us to experience the sensation of touch; and eyes that offer us the wonders of the world around us, to name a few. We can smell the good and the not-so-savory. Within us is a magical symphony of vessels, nerves, cells, and organs that harmoniously work together, sustaining life, and granting us the experience of existence itself. We can cook, laugh, cry, pat a pet, give hugs, and make decisions! Think back for a moment to a time when you were in ill health—perhaps, you were struck down with COVID or a stomach bug. In those moments, our only wish is simply to regain your well-being. Thus, never overlook this aspect; our health and bodies are not a given. It's a gift that should be cherished, nurtured, and celebrated every single day.

For many of us, struggling with poor health or the loss of a sense or limb forms part of our daily reality. Perhaps, you have lost your hearing, but you can celebrate the fact that you still have your eyesight. Perhaps, you have lost a limb; be grateful for the ingenious minds behind prosthetics that enable you to enjoy the gift of independent movement. Direct your focus towards the positive. Consider the awe-inspiring achievements of Paralympic athletes, for instance. Their determination serves as a testament to strength, resilience, gratitude, and the boundless potential that exists within each of us.

Exercise

Being grateful for your body and your health is a way of honoring and valuing yourself. This powerful gesture of gratitude is also an act of self-love, acceptance, and appreciation.

Being able to say thank you to your body is one of the most transformative and significant things you can do, especially if you want to live a more fulfilled, happy life. There is a tiny catch though; it's not always one of the easiest things to do. Society often conditions us to constantly strive for an unattainable standard of perfection, urging us to constantly change to better fit a predetermined mold. And the problem with this? We all have our own blueprint. Our imperfections are the very essence of our perfectly imperfect selves—our own unique beauty. We are overlooking the fact that our imperfections are exactly what contributes to our imperfect perfection. The only mainstream concept that should be enforced in this regard is self-love and body acceptance. Once again, gratitude is your gateway to these invaluable gifts!

Let's take a look at a few aspects to be grateful for when it comes to your health and body:

- I consciously choose and am deeply grateful for my happiness because it profoundly benefits my health.

- I am grateful for my healthy, robust body which serves as a vessel to navigate through life.

- I am grateful that I prioritize being fit, healthy, and in shape.

- I rejoice in the ability to see myself and experience the world through my beautiful eyes.

- I am grateful for every breath I can take, granting me the gift of life.

- I love my quirky, amusing toes.

- I appreciate my fuller figure; it contributes to my unique identity.

- I am grateful that I am happy and content in my own skin.

- I am grateful for my ability to smile, knowing that it radiates and spreads positivity.

- I am happy that I have a healthy, beating heart.

- I am grateful that I can take proactive steps towards improving my health.

- I am grateful that I can freely move around with ease.

- I am so happy that I can enjoy the sound of laughter.

- It's a blessing to be able to hear my voice, making it possible for me to communicate effectively.

Strategies

- Focus on your body's capabilities: We all tend to focus on appearance—it's a common occurrence. However, it can help, especially if acceptance is a challenge, to begin by focusing on appreciating how your body tirelessly functions and what it does for you every day.

- Keep your affirmations realistic: It's not only about positive affirmation; it's also about using *relatable* affirmations. This means that your affirmations should be grounded, reminding you of the practical benefits your body provides to you.

- Health care should be based on self-care: A lot of the time you want to hit the gym or embark on a new diet because you want to improve your physical appearance. There's nothing wrong with that, but perhaps, shifting your perspective could lead to a more enriching outcome. Rather than approaching diet and exercise as ways to improve your body, see them as conscious decisions to nurture and support your body instead.

- Feeling should be the focus: It's not always all about what you see, it's about what you feel. Thus, close your eyes and conduct a body scan from the crown of your head right down to the tips of your toes. Focus on every sensation coursing through every part of your body. It's an objective experience with no judgments, only the experience of every sensation. This unbiased experience serves as a reliable way to cultivate profound gratitude for your body and overall health.

- It's okay to not feel okay: You're not a robot, and there will be days when you're feeling your best. Don't hide and bottle up these emotions. Simply reflect and hone in on the positives. If positivity feels overwhelming and too much to aim for at times, try leaning into a sense of neutrality. View your body or health as neither positive nor negative.

The list is truly endless when it comes to reasons for being grateful for your body and your health. Imagine what you would look like without your skin: Quite a sight, right? Or without your bones and joints, you would be reduced to a blob! You possess the incredible ability to reason and think; you have eyes and arms! And never overlook the power of your beautiful smile—one of the best ways to express gratitude for each and every remarkable aspect of your unique body and health.

Chapter 8:

Day 7—Nature

Daily gratitude is a fountain of blessings. –Lailah Gifty Akita

Go ahead, as with every other day, and work through your list, adding 10 extra gratitude gems. Draw from what you've learned thus far, appreciating your family, relationships, health, and body. Don't forget to pause and pay attention to the things you can be grateful for throughout your day. And of course, last but most certainly not least, end your day with gratitude.

On the list for today, as our added extra, it's all about the great outdoors. Yes, we are going to hone in on why and how we should be grateful for the abundance of nature that envelops us. Let's face it, where would we be without nature? The natural world we find ourselves in is truly an incredible marvel that is nothing short of inspirational. This is the very foundation of our existence! Think of the plants, forests, rivers, oceans, and soil that provide us with air to breathe, food to eat, and water to drink.

Amidst the hustle and bustle of our fast-paced lives, we can so easily lose sight of what is truly important. Unfortunately, most of the time the things we tend to overlook are the things that truly matter such as friendship, true happiness, and good health, to name a few. Nature, in its wondrous way, serves as our grounding force, reminding us to be grateful for these positive aspects that form such an integral part of our lives. Aside from this, our beautiful Earth grants us the opportunity to venture out and interact with an array of other living entities such as the serene trees, vibrant tropical fish, and quirky lizards, right through to majestic giraffes! Each encounter is an opportunity to appreciate all the extraordinary facets of nature.

But nature provides us with more than just these essentials; it plays a pivotal role in our overall physical and mental well-being as well. Nature impacts our economy, from tourism and leisure right through to forestry and farming. Take nature out of the equation, and we will find ourselves within a barren void.

Exercise

Set aside a mere five minutes. Whether you look out a window, take a walk around your garden, go for a brisk stroll on the beach, or bask in the sun, immerse yourself in nature.

Be fully present in the moment as you absorb every little aspect of nature that surrounds you. Take in the crisp, fresh air; listen to the myriad of sounds that serenade you; look at all the colors and shapes; and touch the different textures—all imbued with a comforting sense of grounding. Look at the profound, pure source of life that surrounds you.

Even research has demonstrated the positive impact of nature on our overall well-being. It has been shown that those who spend more time connected with nature tend to be happier and experience a heightened sense of purpose (Weir, 2020). In our modern world, we have become increasingly reliant on technology, spending less time outdoors and more time with our faces glued to screens. This makes it even more important to take the time out and bond as well as appreciate nature, fostering more positive emotions such as creativity, joy, calmness, and concentration. Think of your time spent being grateful for nature as a protective salve for your bustling brain, benefiting both your physical and emotional well-being.

How can we express our gratitude for the abundant gifts that nature bestows upon us?

- Be grateful for the warm kiss of the sun's gentle rays upon your cheeks.

- Be grateful for the snow-clad mountains allowing you to test your skiing prowess or make snow angels.

- Be grateful for the array of shapes, smells, and colors that surround you when the world bursts into bloom.

- Be grateful for the whistling wind that dries your clothes and carries the seeds, fostering new life around you.

- Be grateful for the undulating hills, dense forests, and vast desert landscapes that sculpt the world we live in.

- Be grateful for every living creature, contributing to the rich tapestry of life.

- Be grateful for the rain that quenches the thirst of every living entity.

- Be grateful for every sunrise and sunset that guides you through each day.

- Be grateful for the ground you stand on, which provides the bedrock for all living things.

- Be grateful for the clouds and stars that fill the sky, painting a picture for our eyes.

- Be grateful for every passing season, signifying the rhythm of life itself.

Strategies

Let's explore some strategies for fully immersing yourself in nature and finding your profound sense of gratitude:

- Create your own mini outdoor adventure, and set up a tent in your backyard.

- Seek out shapes in the canvas of passing clouds or stars.

- Leap into puddles after a shower of refreshing rain.

- Step outside, and dance in the rain.

- Plant a tree, or nurture your garden.

- Take off your shoes, and relish in the sensation of the earth beneath your feet.

- Prepare a delectable picnic, whether in a park or your own backyard.

- Identify things in nature such as birds, trees, or flowers.

- Join a hiking group to explore and appreciate nature with like-minded people.

- Practice mindfulness through yoga or meditation outdoors.

- Paint a picturesque landscape inspired by nature.

- Take an invigorating dip in a lake, river, or ocean.

- Collect items outdoors that remind you of nature's beauty.

- Cultivate your own bounty of fruits, veggies, or herbs.

- Draw some pictures, or build some castles in the sand that the waves or rains will eventually wash over.

What better way could there possibly be to combat stress, anxiety, and fatigue? When you spend time in nature, you allow your attention and focus to flow effortlessly, granting yourself an opportunity to filter out all the many distractions that you are faced with in daily life.

Being grateful for nature is a way to stay grounded, acting as an anchor that reminds us of the significance we play in this intricate, wondrous journey known as life.

Chapter 9:

Day 8—Gratitude for Things

Acknowledging the good that you already have in your life is the foundation for all abundance. –Eckhart Tolle

You've got it! Expand on your list, incorporating the aspects we have worked through. Take moments to pause, look around, and embrace gratitude. And to cap off your day, sprinkle it with a generous dose of gratitude!

Today, we are going to focus on an item that we own, something that's a bit weathered—maybe, it's prone to frequent mishaps, or perhaps, it's in need of an upgrade. We all have that one thing—perhaps, more than one—that we wish we could replace with a similar, shinier, grander version. My car is a great example. It's not a Ferrari, but it gets me where I need to be. While I do, at times, entertain the idea of an upgrade, I still recognize and am grateful for its value. It serves its purpose. There are plenty of people who live without the convenience of having their own car as a means of transport.

Let's take another example. Consider a watch: Some own a watch worth as much as a down payment on a home, while others sport a watch that costs merely a few dollars. However, irrespective of what that watch cost, they all tell the same time. You see, society constantly bombards us with messages that tell us we need more, promising that things will elevate our lives or status. Strangely enough, we buy into it, only to end up feeling inadequate if we can not attain these things.

With the onslaught of social media, the situation is exacerbated, fostering envy and a culture of constant comparison, even if we know that what we see is not the full truth! It slowly chips away at our self-worth and erodes our happiness. Then, it just snowballs and, we end up thinking life is unfair—that what we have is not good enough and outdated. What happens? We end up buying and paying for things that we either don't truly need or can't truly afford. Well, you most certainly do *not* need to keep up with this rat race. All you need to do is pause and readjust your perspective.

Exercise

Take a moment and consider this item that you have, wishing you could upgrade. Ask yourself in which way this item contributes to your life, irrespective of its current state or condition. How does it make your life easier?

Perhaps, it's your home. Maybe, it's not the ideal abode with the white picket fence you once imagined, but for now, it provides you with shelter, keeping you warm in winter and dry when it rains. It's your own personal sanctuary, where you return after a long day, allowing you to recharge for the next. Think of all the homeless people, feeling vulnerable and exposed, who would give anything to have even a day of what you have. Be grateful for your home; be grateful for your warm bed and invigorating shower. Cherish the feeling of walking through your front door.

Do you the days when we needed some spare change to make a call from a public phone and lacked a camera that could instantly capture and show us our remarkable moments? Be grateful for that outdated smartphone of yours, making life a whole lot easier and countless things more accessible. No more fumbling for change or waiting a week for a roll of film to be developed.

Always take a moment to appreciate the things that serve their purpose, which are often overlooked yet truly valuable in our lives:

- I am grateful for my reliable car that takes me wherever I need to be.

- I appreciate my trusty old television, allowing me to cuddle up and enjoy some inspiring shows.

- I am grateful for my home; it's a cherished haven that provides me with safety and shelter.

- I am grateful for my old phone, which still keeps me in touch with my loved ones.

- I value my inexpensive watch, which faithfully keeps me informed of the time.

- I am grateful for the well-used tennis racket that enables me to spend some good, healthy time with friends outdoors.

- I am grateful for my old tea set that still serves up a warm, hearty cup of tea for me to enjoy.

- I value my enduring coat, worn year after year, keeping me snug and warm through the winters.

- I am grateful for my dependable, old stove that continues to prepare delicious, nourishing meals.

- I am truly grateful for my aging sound system, still serenading me with beautiful music to dance to.

- I am grateful for the budget-friendly pen that enables me to take notes and sign important documents.

Strategies

- Gain perspective: Think of something you have and that you take for granted. It could be your outdated laptop for instance. What challenges do people face without that item you take for granted?

- Don't be picky: Value absolutely *all* aspects that enhance your life, no matter how big, small, old, or outdated they are. Accept each aspect for what it is, and express gratitude. There is nothing too old or outdated for you to be grateful for.

- Stop comparing: No need to compare yourself to others. Your self-worth and fulfillment do not hinge on external factors. Your essence as a person is not defined by what you own. And if you have a competitive streak, compete against your own progress. Are you a better person today than you were yesterday?

- Do a social media detox: Frequent exposure to the carefully curated highlights of other people's lives can undoubtedly lead to dissatisfaction in your own life. Constantly scrolling can easily suck anyone into a void of endless comparison, highlighting what we might perceive ourselves as lacking. But do we truly lack these things? Would these things genuinely be life-changing? Doing a regular social media detox once in a while is most certainly recommended. It allows you to refocus on the positive aspects that are already present in your life, highlighting your abundance instead of creating the illusion of scarcity.

- Want versus need: How many of the things we desire do we truly need? Ask yourself if what you desire is truly necessary for your well-being. To appreciate what you have, you need to recognize the disparity between what you need and what you want. Appreciating what you already have acknowledges your progress and propels you forward.

As you smile while you think of these things, you will find yourself becoming happy with what you already have, allowing yourself to step out of a mindset of lack and scarcity. Know that you can upgrade these items in due time. For now, at least, you have them and they serve you well, even if they aren't the latest and greatest.

Also remember, as the day winds down, to end it with a grateful heart and a happy smile!

Chapter 10:

Day 9—Work

We should certainly count our blessings, but we should also make our blessings count. –Neal A. Maxwell

Welcome to the rollover into Day 10! And please, don't hold back; delve into those gratitude treasures. Expand your list, adding more aspects to be grateful for. Take some time out throughout the day, keeping an eye on the things to be grateful for, and remember, round your day out with yet another hearty dose of gratitude.

For our task today, we are going to focus on reasons to be grateful for our work. Now, when it comes to work, there are two vastly different scenarios: On one hand, there are the fortunate souls who love what they do for a living. They earn their income by pursuing their passions! Then, there's the flip side of the coin, which unfortunately will resonate with most. Work is just a job, a mere means to pay the bills, a soul-draining task to make ends meet. The latter scenario is rather a sticky situation, as it's never just one reason that makes work feel burdensome, but rather an accumulation of factors. Some may resent the commute to work, dislike their colleagues, or even have a tyrant as a boss. The hours could feel grueling, and the salary may not reflect your efforts—a typical situation some describe as "maximum input, minimum wage." And the clencher? Without a job, you have no income, and as much as you dislike it, it's a lifeline at the end of the day.

However, all is not lost; you need a shift in perspective. Consider that paycheck you receive that enables you to pay the bills: Think of the food and clothes you can afford, keeping you comfortable. Think of the birthday gift you could buy to put a smile on someone's face. Perhaps, you could even treat yourself to a holiday, a nice dinner, or a night at the movies. Think about the many people who go to bed hungry, cold, and desperate. Think of the people who can't afford the basic necessities in life. Consider those who can't mark a birthday, afford a pair of new shoes, or even enjoy a warm bath.

Shifting your perspective will allow you to appreciate the stability and opportunities your work provides.

Exercise

So, what's there to do in order to change perspective? You need to recognize the value in every little thing that holds a presence in your life. Every aspect and facet of life is there for you to learn from and expand. Next time those feelings of doom, gloom, and ungratefulness start creeping in, look for three things you can be grateful for about your job. I guarantee you that if you take a moment to reflect, you will most certainly find at least three good reasons. When you transition your thoughts from dreading work to appreciating the job you have, you'll notice a significant boost in your happiness.

Next time your boss comes down on you, pause and take a deep breath before you allow your anger and frustration to run away with you. Remember: "I am very grateful for my job. It supports me financially and gives me something to do."

In discovering your gratitude for your work, the following may be of assistance:

- Think of some valuable relationships you have fostered through your job. Some of these connections are important as they significantly contribute to your overall experience.

- Consider yourself fortunate if you receive valuable health benefits as part of your job package.

- Recognize the significance of your contribution to your job, especially if it involves helping others.

- Perhaps, you are privileged enough to work outdoors and not be confined to a desk.

- Maybe, you have a great annual bonus you can look forward to as a little extra motivation to keep you going.

- Maybe, your current job is a stepping stone to greater things, unlocking your potential to achieve something more significant.

- Think of the privilege you have to improve and showcase your skills every single day, allowing you to expand and improve.

Strategies

- Be sure to take regular breaks: What better way to spend that time than with a few moments of practicing mindfulness and gratitude? This will allow you to step away from any moments of overwhelm and reshift your focus.

- Organize your workspace: Having a workspace that is organized and tidy will most certainly contribute to a more relaxed and controlled environment where you will find it easier to boost your productivity, express gratitude, and experience peacefulness.

- Keep work at work: While occasional overtime is unavoidable, it shouldn't become a regular thing. Likewise, you should generally avoid communicating about work, such as answering emails, outside of working hours. Balancing your work and personal life is crucial for maintaining healthy relationships and mental well-being.

- Look for purpose: We all have moments when work is not enjoyable. However, to unlock some gratitude, be sure to regularly remind yourself of why you work. Consider your contribution to the team; perhaps, you offer valuable advice or bring positivity with a joke and a smile.

- Smile and engage: Create a deeper meaning, and make your work more enjoyable by fostering good relationships with your coworkers. Having a positive attitude and stronger bonds with your coworkers helps cultivate a more positive outlook toward your work.

- Upgrade your skill set: Sometimes, a lack of fulfillment at work could be indicative that you are in need of a new challenge. Upgrading your skills brings a fresh sense of purpose and motivation to your life.

Whether you're a boss or an employee, nobody's job is perfect. On top of this, you have to remember that we, as humans, have this knack: a bias toward negativity, giving more weight to problems than successes. Yes, pain affects us more than positivity, but there is always something to appreciate in your current situation, you just need to pay attention to the details. You need to look at the situation through the lens of gratitude; this is what will allow you to get the full story and not just focus on the negatives.

Remember to end your day with gratitude and keep smiling. You're capable of more than you think!

Chapter 11:

Day 10—Take a Break

In life, one has a choice to take one of two paths: to wait for some special day or to celebrate each special day. –Rasheed Ogunlaru

Keep up the great work, just like you do every day! Expand your gratitude list with 10 additional aspects to be grateful for, and sprinkle gratitude throughout your day. And lastly, before you call it a night, wrap it up with a wholesome dose of gratitude.

For today, you will be required to carve out some time for yourself to take a break, reflect, and appreciate all the various aspects of your life. Whether it's a peaceful garden stroll, a leisurely cup of tea, or simply watching the world go by, choose what brings you joy, tranquility, and a sense of gratitude. You see, in our fast-paced lives, we tend to constantly run from one chore to another, one deadline to the next, racing to check off as much as we can on our never-ending to-do lists. There are school drop-offs, weekend errands, and get-togethers. So much to do and so little time! Thus, taking time out is a very rare occurrence in most of our lives—almost a luxury, one could say. This is not supposed to be a luxury; taking time out for yourself should be non-negotiable.

Taking regular breaks is not just about sitting still and zoning out. It's necessary for your brain to reset and recharge. Of course, we have to keep up the grind. However, without taking regular breaks for yourself, you can severely negatively impact your mental health and performance. If you need to refocus, take a break. Feeling absent-minded and experiencing some brain fog? Take a breather. Perhaps, you're in need of a creative spark or a fresh solution? Yes, take a break. The key thing to remember is that taking a break doesn't entail you getting all caught up in a different tedious task. It should be infused with a sense of playfulness to lighten your mood, igniting inspiration and motivation.

Exercise

Find something that you like to do that brings you a sense of fulfillment, relaxation, and joy. Try and dedicate some time to this every day, and really bask in the gratitude to allow yourself to properly reset and fully recharge.

At the end of the day, there is no one-size-fits-all when it comes to taking breaks. Some days it might be completely impossible to squeeze in a break or two, while on other days, you might feel that you don't need one at all. Then, there will be the days that you will be eagerly looking forward to that bit of "me time." Trust your instincts, and take your breaks based on how you feel. When you feel emotionally, physically, or mentally drained, hit pause on the clock to nourish and nurture yourself. Also, keep a keen eye on these cues throughout the day; our moods can shift with the circumstances we face. Be wary of those energy dips.

Sometimes, a break can merely require you to step away for a few moments from a given task at hand to ground yourself again. And what better way to make the most of these moments of rejuvenation than by practicing the art of gratitude? After all, it's one of the most powerful tools you freely have at your disposal when it comes to recharging your batteries!

- Engage in meditation or other mindfulness practices.

- Go for a stroll.

- Tidy up a part of your house.

- Do some light stretching for a few minutes.

- Make yourself a healthy treat.

- Take an invigorating shower.

- Call a loved one.

- Engage in a quick workout to boost your energy levels.

- Enjoy a cup of coffee or tea.

- Journal or doodle.

- Simply stare out of your window.

- Read a couple of pages from a book.

- Express yourself through playing music or engaging in any other art form.

Strategies

- Observe your energy levels throughout the day, and do regular check-ins with yourself. Ask yourself, " How am I feeling?"

- Pay attention to what your mind and body are telling you. Notice how they are operating: Are they at full capacity, or are you experiencing a sense of burnout?

- Take a moment to gauge your mood first thing in the morning. If you wake up and feel stressed, fatigued, or agitated, it most certainly is a sign that you will benefit from regular breaks throughout the day.

- Forget social pressure; don't let it dictate your priorities, especially when it comes to your mental health. Put yourself first.

- If you notice any negative feelings such as being overwhelmed or frustrated, remember that it's perfectly okay to take that break and return after a bit of reflection. This is a powerful strategy that will make you more responsive instead of reactive in a given situation, allowing you to handle it with more clarity and grace.

- Taking a moment to practice deep breathing is a wonderful way to pause and reconnect with yourself. When coupled with a sense of gratitude, focusing on deep-breathing exercises becomes a powerful method to nurture patience, infuse tranquility, and ground yourself.

We are not sure of what each day will bring; life's filled with surprises and no guarantees. But, one thing is certain, and that is the fact that we are all on this journey called life together. Sometimes, we are confronted with experiences—such as the loss of a loved one—that force us to pause and reflect, questioning our existence: Why are we doing what we're doing, and what significance does it hold? However, amidst the daily chaos of life, we need not wait for these moments to bring us to a halt in order to reflect, realign, and appreciate life itself. We can seize these moments regularly, scattered throughout the day or week. Breaks come in all shapes and sizes, depending on what you require at that given point in time. Some breaks are extended, such as holidays; some are brief intervals. Irrespective of which break you take, make sure that it is something that occurs often enough to benefit your mental and physical health. Breaks offer you a space to rest amidst the rush of ambitions and to-do lists.

And remember, wrap up your day with a generous dose of gratitude and a matching smile!

Chapter 12:

Day 11—Reflect and Say Thank You (People in Your Past)

No one who achieves success does so without the help of others. The wise and confident acknowledge this help with gratitude. – Alfred North Whitehead

No surprises here, you're on the right track! Dive deeper, and further expand on your gratitude list. Remember, it's perfectly fine if some aspects overlap. It's all up to you and make it as meaningful and personal as possible. Then, as you go through your day, take regular intervals to experience the warmth of gratitude, and before you drift off to dreamland, end your day with gratitude.

For today, you will have to focus on three individuals who've had a profound impact on your life. So, who are these special people who had such a significant role in your life? The next question is why? In general, these people have brought about positive, transformative changes in your life. This guiding light could have come in any form, whether it be support or guidance. These people were movers and shakers, spreading their knowledge and uplifting others—climbing their own mountains and lending a hand to others on their way up. You will most likely find, upon reflection, that these people share some striking traits. This could include dedicating themselves to what gives their lives purpose, staying committed to continual self-improvement, and their power to create positive change. They use their influence for the greater good.

These people are a wellspring of inspiration and upliftment, even in memory. They operated from their hearts with genuine care and compassion, fully aware of the impact they could make. Their influence was an honor, accepted with grace. They are the strong pillars in your life that have provided you with constructive feedback, empowering you to be the best version of yourself. These are authentic, supportive relationships that form part of the bedrock of who you are today.

Exercise

There is undoubtedly a myriad of people that you have crossed paths with in life, each leaving their mark and playing a significant part in helping you become the person you are today.

For now, your job is to narrow it down to three of these individuals. Take a moment, and jot down all the reasons you are grateful for their contributions to your life. Yet again, you can pen this down in a heartfelt letter dedicated to them, or simply reflect on it quietly through your mind's eye. Please, keep in mind that, sometimes, these people do not always tick all the boxes as we talked about earlier. In some cases, it could be the challenging situations that you were exposed to through this particular individual that have led to significant positive changes in your life. Let's look at an example: Perhaps, you had a partner who struggled with alcohol abuse, which led you to a program that introduced you to a new support system, wonderful friends, and a deeper understanding of your own struggles. Or perhaps, the schoolyard bully profoundly impacted you in such a way that you started your own movement against bullying, helping to raise awareness and safeguard others.

What truly matters with this exercise is that these people sparked something within you that was so strong that it propelled you toward a greater version of yourself. They are your catalysts for expansion in being extraordinary.

- Your parents could have impacted your life significantly, for better or worse. But think of what empowered you, what you gained from the situation that turned you into a better version of yourself. Be grateful for the strength you have gained.

- Your siblings could have perhaps been a great source of support, guiding you through the wandering journey of life, always on the lookout, making you wiser and more prepared for the road ahead.

- Maybe, you could be grateful for your teachers and coaches throughout your life, influencing and educating you to become a more resilient adult. Perhaps, they instilled in you that life is an ever-evolving journey filled with lessons that should be appreciated and put forth for improvement.

- You could be grateful for that loyal school friend who helped shape you into fostering and appreciating valuable bonds with others.

- Or maybe, there was a stranger who crossed your path and treated you with such kindness at a time when you needed it the most, opening you up to the greatness of humanity again.

- Hey, you might even consider that bully at work who acted as the driving force behind your career change, prompting you to step out into the great unknown and seek better, brighter horizons.

- You could have had a grandparent who shared some profound wisdom and insights with you, shaping the way you think and make valuable decisions.

Strategies

- Pay it forward: Reflecting on the lessons and strength that our mentors and guides imparted, and then passing that wisdom on to others, is a beautiful way of ensuring you spread the goodwill. Pay it forward: Reflecting on the lessons and strength our mentors and guides imparted, and then passing that wisdom on to others, is a beautiful way of ensuring you spread the goodwill.

- Live in their honor: These special people who have impacted your life would want you to be happy and live the fulfilled life you deserve with the lessons they imparted. Thus, live each day to the fullest, taking in every aspect with gratitude and an open perspective, recognizing all the abundance that surrounds you.

- Hang on to a keepsake: Keep something that reminds you of this person to trigger some inspiration. This will also act as a reminder to express gratitude, not only towards them but for all the other things in your life you have to be grateful for.

- Care for what they care about: Living according to the values that they instilled within you is a powerful way to express gratitude. Engage in activities that they hold dear. This could be anything from volunteering for a cause they support right through to adopting one of their favorite hobbies. Honoring them in creative ways is a wonderful nudge to remind you to be grateful for their presence in your life.

Embracing gratitude for these profound individuals in your life allows not only you but also others to come together in celebration; this also provides you with solace if they are not physically with you anymore. And don't forget to share your favorite memories and stories of them, ensuring that their essence is cherished, perpetuating their legacy, and paying homage to the extraordinary person they were.

Of course, this should all be done with a radiant smile and retiring for the day with a heart filled with gratitude!

Chapter 13:

Day 12—Strangers on the

Street

The only people with whom you should try to get even are those who have helped you. –John E. Southard

The gratitude show must go on through your gratitude practice. Continue with your list, add more items, pause, and be grateful throughout your day. And your final curtain call for the day should be done with a healthy dose of gratitude.

Today's spotlight is on strangers. I know, I know, it does sound a bit peculiar at first, but trust me, it all forms part of the gratitude puzzle. We are blessed with all sorts of people in this world. There are so many we never even see or get to meet face-to-face, yet their influence on our lives is rather profound. Think about the garbage collectors who diligently make their rounds to collect your trash, the unsung supermarket shelf stockers, the hardworking engineers who pave our roads, and the skilled plumbers who ensure you have a regular supply of clean water. What about the friendly face behind the counter at your corner store or the bus driver who safely gets you to work? Let us not forget the pilots, firefighters, police officers, and countless others who serve us on a daily basis, often without us realizing it or perhaps even giving it a second thought.

We so easily overlook the significance of a lot of these roles, but where would we be without these people? Each and every person has a place and a purpose in this world, forming part of a greater collective that enables us to live our lives. Every single one deserves to be cherished and respected for their invaluable contributions. After all, aren't we all infinitely connected in this tapestry called life? Thus, let's acknowledge them with a heart full of gratitude!

Exercise

While you are out and about today, make a conscious effort to thank people. Oh yes, look them in the eye, give them a warm smile, be sincere, and say thank you.

You see, gratitude comes full circle when it's both reflective and expressive, which means it is not just confined to your mind or journal, but it's also a very powerful expression you share with others. Gratitude plays a vital role when it comes to forming meaningful, cooperative connections. Think back to the last time a stranger thanked you: Can you recall how great that made you feel? It probably boosted your sense of worth, making you feel more empowered. Isn't it rather an odd occurrence that so many of us will go the extra mile to lodge a complaint if we're not happy with something, but we rarely make the effort of saying thank you and celebrating when things go right? Well, that's a whole different story. Perhaps, it's that infamous negativity bias of ours that comes into play here.

Here's a beautiful take on gratitude: the find, remind, and bind theory. According to psychologist Sara Algoe, this theory points to gratitude being such a social powerhouse that it helps us find new relationships, reminds us of our existing relationships, and assists us in nurturing all these relationships (*If You Want to Feel...*, 2022).

So, let's look at how you can find and bind a couple of new relationships:

- Walking the kids to school? Take a moment to thank the wonderful crossing attendants for playing a crucial role in keeping your kids safe.

- If you are lodging a complaint, remember the person on the other side of the line is there to assist you; they are not to blame for the issue that arose. These people are merely there doing their jobs and earning a living, just like you. Hey, maybe they don't even enjoy doing what they're doing. Make sure to take a moment and thank them for assisting you.

- What about those referees at your children's sporting events? In general, a lot of these people volunteer their time for the benefit of all the kids involved. If there is a wrong call made, remember that mistakes happen and nobody is perfect. At least, they are dedicating their time to the betterment of the community. Be grateful for them before frustration kicks in.

- Thank the cashier at the supermarket. Your gratitude and acknowledgment will make them feel valued, helping set a positive tone for the rest of their day.

- Perhaps, someone shared a sad story with you. Thank them for sharing their vulnerability with you, and be grateful for the trust and connection that's established.

- How about the janitors at your local gym, keeping things in tip-top hygienic condition, contributing to your health and overall well-being?

- Think about all the security guards working tirelessly to help keep our communities safe, making it easier for us to move around freely and safely.

- Don't forget the maintenance crews at our parks working hard to keep the natural spaces well-groomed. This allows you to reconnect with and enjoy nature whenever the need arises.

Strategies

- You can write a positive review about the service, business, or person from a specific institution.

- Make cookies, send a pizza, or buy some coffee for people in helping professions that facilitate your daily life. This could be a teacher, healthcare provider, police officer, or even a refuse worker, to name a few.

- Donate some clothes, toys, and other useful items.

- Pay for the person behind you in the supermarket or drive-through.

- Leave a big tip with a special note at your favorite restaurant.

- Hold the door for a stranger.

- Help someone carry or load their groceries.

- Invite a stranger to join you for a meal, or simply buy a meal for someone in need.

- Distribute care packages for caregivers.

- Anonymously leave care packages on someone's doorstep.

- Ask to talk to the manager, and compliment the staff member who always diligently waits on you.

- Call the "How's my driving?" number on the back of a service vehicle, and compliment the driver.

- Or you can simply just say thank you face-to-face to a specific person.

These are just a few examples to get you off to a great start! It's incredible how many different people in various different careers play a vital role in our daily lives. A simple "thank you" goes a long way. It spreads love, care, empathy, and gratitude. The world is filled with incredible individuals. Try and thank as many people as you can today. Look them in the eye, share that warm smile, and let them experience the warmth of gratitude. This simple fact holds the power to make the world a better place!

Remember to end your day with gratitude and keep smiling!

Chapter 14:

Day 13—Mistakes

Whether you think you can or think you can't, you're right. –Henry Ford

Start by expanding on your list and adding those additional gratitude gems. Don't forget to sprinkle gratitude throughout the day. Lastly, as the day comes to a close, top it off with one more generous dose of gratitude.

Now, let's talk about mistakes. Nobody's perfect, we all make mistakes, and might I add, perfection is overrated in the first place. Allow me to let you in on a little secret: Mistakes are not the end of the world. Well, of course, it's all dependant on how you perceive them. In general, we have this tendency to beat ourselves up over the mistakes we make. We end up dwelling on them, clinging to the past, being consumed by the future, and overlooking the abundance of opportunities that surround us in the present. Maybe, you said something you wish you hadn't or slipped up at work causing a financial hiccup. Worst of the worst, perhaps you forgot a loved one's birthday! It doesn't matter what the specifics are, we have all been there. But what's important during these times is to take a moment and reflect on what mistakes mean to you. How do you typically respond when you make one?

Interestingly enough, Jason S. Moser from Michigan State University points out a key difference between those who believe intelligence can be developed and those who think it's fixed: how they respond to mistakes (Moser et al., 2011)! If you believe that you can learn and grow from your mistakes, you will most certainly handle the aftermath much more successfully compared to those who perceive mistakes as a final judgment. Thus, the game aims to shift your perspective when it comes to mistakes. Next time a blunder of some sort occurs, take a step back, analyze what went wrong, and figure out what there is to learn from it. This will allow you to piece together what has just transpired. You'll be better equipped to respond in the future or even prevent the same mistake from happening again. It's best to be responsive instead of reactive.

You see, mistakes are a blend of lessons and blessings in disguise; think of them as "blessons." They are not life sentences; you are too vast and unique as an individual to be defined by just a mere moment in life. Mistakes allow you to gain knowledge, even if it's negative. Indeed, those lessons can be tough at times, but they still enhance your learning process. They form an inevitable, integral part of life in general. When you recognize and own your mistakes, you expand as a person. They help you regain control in situations by pointing out where there is room for improvement, leading you down new pathways of exploration, and allowing you to venture out into the great unknown.

Embrace them. I understand, at the moment, it is easier said than done. But shifting your perspective to see it as a journey towards improvement will allow you to better appreciate these moments of misjudgment. Remember, nobody is immune to making mistakes; they are all part of our continual growth and evolution as people. As they say, you can run but you can't hide!

Exercise

Take a stroll down memory lane, and revisit some of your past blunders. Look at them through fresh eyes, and approach them with an objective perspective. Hunt for the lessons hidden within these experiences. You can jot them down or say them out loud; it's a personal experience. At the end of the day, the purpose of this exercise is to turn those personal negatives into positives, helping you find gratitude even in the not-so-pleasant moments of life.

Think back to childhood when the primary way of learning was through making mistakes. Let's take walking for instance: You didn't just get up out of bed one morning and miraculously start walking straight away. No, you went through trial and error, stumbling and getting back up until those first steps became a reality. Then, perhaps, you had to learn how to ride a bicycle. How many times did you wobble, tumble, stumble, and become the teary-eyed owner of a couple of bruises before successfully peddling along on your own? And let's not forget the challenges that came with learning how to read and write! How many times in life have you had to go through trial and error to master a skill? Plenty! But that's exactly how you learned and grew as a person, right? And I am sure that you may agree that the moral of this story is not just limited to childhood.

Now, here's another important aspect to keep your eyes on when it comes to making mistakes in life: your self-talk. Yes, a lot of us have a tendency to engage in negative self-talk when we err. This only amplifies the weight of the mistake, blinding us to the valuable lessons waiting to be embraced. Think about it, talking to yourself in a demeaning manner is most certainly not going to fix the problem or make it disappear. In fact, it will only drag you further down into the depths of despair. That's rather counterproductive in the quest for gratitude, isn't it?

So, the next time you make a mistake, instead of taking a subjective dive into self-criticism, try to be objective and learn from the situation. It's merely a moment that's nudging you towards a sprinkle of self-reflection. Analyze it, and see what went wrong; it's a step towards improvement. Think of it as your first step in the right direction. Never forget that the ability to learn and grow is most certainly something to always be grateful for. Embrace it!

So, what exactly do we do when we step back and reflect? We simply objectively question the situation. Remember, there's no judgment required here, only gratitude:

- What can I learn from this situation or my mistake?

- Is there someone who can help me understand what I need to learn?

- What can I do to pick myself up and move on from this mistake in the most productive way?

- Is there something I could have done differently, and if so, what is it, and what would those expected outcomes be?

- Do I need to improve any of my skills?

- What is the good that I can take from this failure?

- In the grander scheme of things, how big is this mistake?

- How did my actions affect me?

- How did my actions affect others?

- Are there people that I should apologize to?

- What are the consequences of this experience that I would not want to repeat?

- What other different approaches could I take if the same or a similar situation arises in the future?

- Was I reactive or responsive during the situation?

- Am I going to allow this situation to engulf me and happen to me, or am I going to learn from it?

Strategies

- Reframe and analyze: It is very important that you shift your perspective when it comes to mistakes. Start seeing them as learning processes instead of final judgment calls. Put a dedicated effort into stepping back from the situation, allowing yourself to see the bigger picture. Work through the questions we revised. I can guarantee you that some life answers will pop up amid this reflection.

- Acknowledge your mistakes: You need to admit when you are wrong, and never attempt to cover anything up. It's a futile attempt because it only delays and prolongs the lesson that should be learned. Aside from that, life will present itself in a different form eventually. Turning a blind eye to your mistakes is akin to a slow poison: You are only adding more stress, anxiety, and confusion to your life. If an apology is needed, don't hesitate to make it, even if it's to yourself. Your honesty and ability to take responsibility speak volumes about your courage. People will remember this over the mishaps.

- Put it into practice: You most certainly did not go through all of this for nothing! You need to take action and claim your growth, learn from your mistakes, adjust, and put it into action. This could mean restrategizing, coming up with more creative solutions, or not overlooking important details to name a few. Practice, practice, and practice what you have learned. Always be grateful for the insight you have gained.

- Remember, you can't avoid mistakes: Alongside death and taxes—yes it's rather gloomy—change is inevitable. Change is what exposes us to the unknown; anything can happen there. It's rather a scary thought, now, isn't it? Your face changes, your garden changes, and technology changes; there is no escape! You are not alone, however, rest assured. Mistakes are most often the catalysts for change. If we change, we grow, but if we don't grow, what happens? For any living entity, down to a plant, we die. Embrace your mistakes; they are gateways to change. Be grateful that you are growing and not dying. Sure, the unfamiliar is scary, but you have to step into it, enabling yourself to transform into the person you were meant to be.

- It's okay: Undoubtedly, making mistakes puts us in a vulnerable position. We feel discouraged, defeated, and overwhelmed. However, keep an open mind; what's the lesson? What can you take from this situation? What's going to make you feel grateful? Only when you understand this perspective can you improve upon yourself and help others to do the same.

- Review and reflect: When you take time out to express gratitude, review and reflect to evaluate your progress. This will highlight where there is room for improvement as well as encourage you to keep going on the path of growth.

The truth is that we all have bad days, so don't be afraid when it comes to making mistakes. It's an integral part of the human experience. Think of it as an opportunity to be grateful for every day that gives you the chance to recalibrate and gather wisdom. When you approach these situations with mindful awareness, they grant you the opportunity for profound self-reflection. Embrace every moment; these moments grant you the opportunity to delve into the depths of your being and properly understand the motives that drive your actions.

With this exercise, you are holding up a mirror to your aspirations and vulnerabilities alike, allowing you to simultaneously be grateful for all aspects of your life. This capacity is a true marvel—a compass that steers you toward a brighter, better version of yourself.

And never forget to conclude your day with a regular dose of gratitude accompanied by a warm, heartfelt smile.

Chapter 15:

Day 14—Yourself!

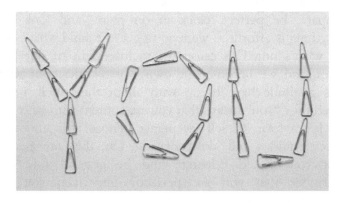

Gratitude is more of a compliment to yourself than someone else. –
Raheel Farooq

Here we are, on Day 14 of our gratitude journey! Simply expand your gratitude list, pause throughout the day, and soak in all the wonderful things you have to be grateful for. Of course, you will have to close your day with that trusted dose of gratitude.

Throughout the course of this journey, have you noticed a shift in your perspective? Perhaps, you are experiencing a greater sense of fulfillment, joy, or satisfaction. Have you noticed that by granting yourself just a few moments to be grateful every day you are nurturing yourself to become filled with deeper contentment? This is because you have found the power within yourself to be grateful for every facet of your life. You are not dependent merely on external factors to dictate your worth and happiness, you find and acknowledge the beauty in everything that surrounds you.

You might be pondering and questioning all the steps, but our journey has brought us to this point: *you*. Sometimes, the biggest challenge we face in our lives is to be grateful for ourselves. In a world where we are forced to stare and compare, be perfect, clock in on point, and look like everything is effortless, we tend to get lost amid what's real and what's not. This causes us to lose sight of our true selves, and we become our own worst critics. But what does gratitude have to do with all of this? Well, being grateful for "you" means that you are content with who you are. It's a form of self-acceptance. Those little annoying aspects, quirks, and idiosyncrasies? Oh, they are exactly what you should celebrate and be grateful for. Just remember that you are perfectly imperfect; you are wonderfully unique! That, in itself, should most certainly be celebrated.

Self-gratitude is a practice where you affirm things about yourself that you value and appreciate. It could be anything, be it your skills, personality traits, talents, style, or knowledge, to name a few. The added bonus of practicing self-gratitude: It works wonders when it comes to silencing negative self-talk. You start seeing yourself in a more positive, empowered light, dramatically improving your self-esteem.

The more you show gratitude towards yourself, the more you will appreciate and cherish who you are, just the way you are.

Exercise

For today, it's all about celebrating you! You will jot down three wonderful things about yourself. You need to hone in on each of these aspects and bask in the powerful sense of gratitude washing over you.

I am sure you are well familiar with the age-old wisdom that you need to love yourself first to love another. That's true! When it comes to love, it has to start within, and that means embracing gratitude for who you are. This helps you highlight all the positive aspects of yourself, recognizing your talents, achievements, beauty, and skills. Gratitude also shows you how to harness these wonderful aspects of yourself to enrich the lives and world around you. When you embrace gratitude for who you are, you enable yourself to make choices that honor your values and uphold your well-being and integrity. Self-gratitude is the fertile ground from which self-love blossoms. And the more you can appreciate and love yourself, the more you will become attuned to all the things around you to be grateful for. It fosters your self-worth and boosts your self-esteem.

Self-gratitude is most certainly not about harboring a sense of superiority. These two concepts are vastly different. Superiority generally stems from a deep-seated feeling of inferiority. Self-gratitude, on the other hand, stems from a place of true appreciation, humility, and an awareness that we are all inherently interconnected. Gratitude is a beautiful dance of giving and receiving—of recognizing both the worthiness of others and yourself.

Now, when it comes to the self, it might be difficult or uncomfortable to find something you are initially grateful for. We are stuck in this mindset where we have to constantly improve and keep up with societal standards, feeling like we have to constantly panel-beat ourselves to fit a certain mold. This is perfectly normal, but it's time for a change though. It's not about changing yourself to conform or fit in anymore; rather, it's about appreciating yourself. Thus, simply start with something easy to be grateful for about yourself. You are worthy of your own love and appreciation.

- I am grateful that I am extremely caring and kind towards animals.

- I am grateful that I am a solution-driven person.

- I am thankful for my resilience and strength, knowing that I will always see things through.

- I am grateful that I am a good, helpful friend to others.

- I am thankful for having the ability to always find the positives in any given situation.

- I appreciate my hunger to constantly learn and expand my knowledge.

- I am grateful for my 10 quirky toes that help me balance and walk around freely every day.

- I love how my hair frames my face and makes my eyes stand out.

- I love the clothes I chose to wear today; they compliment my body beautifully.

- I appreciate my beautiful, unique body that enables me to experience life itself.

- I am thankful for being so proficient in playing the piano.

- I am grateful that I can practice patience and gratitude regularly.

- I am so happy that I am a very creatively expressive person.

- I am truly blessed to be such a math genius.

- I appreciate all the freckles beautifully scattered over my face.

- I am grateful for my sense of style, enabling me to better express myself.

- I love my bushy eyebrows; they make me so unique.

Strategies

- Celebrate yourself, and go buy yourself some flowers, a good book, or a special treat for instance.

- Take a whole day off, and spend time alone, engaging in activities that relax and uplift you.

- Make a list of all the compliments people have given you.

- Spend time in front of the mirror, and thank yourself for all your good qualities, contributions, and accomplishments.

- Take a relaxing, mindful stroll through the garden or a park to ground yourself.

- Get creative, and create gratitude artwork to express yourself.

- Find two positives for every negative complaint you have about yourself.

- Download a gratitude app on your phone.

- Do a social media detox, or clear out any negative accounts, replacing them with more positive ones.

- Spend some extra quality time with loved ones or pets.

- Cook yourself a delicious, hearty meal that you always love or, perhaps, even something new you've always wanted to try.

- Take yourself on a date to the movies.

- Think back to all the times others were grateful for you.

Practicing self-gratitude is not just some superficial ritual. Self-gratitude is a powerful act of self-care and self-love. It is the key that enables you to wholeheartedly love and give to others around you. If your cup is empty, what can you possibly pour into the cups of others?

When you engage in any of these activities, pay close attention to your emotions; feel the warmth of happiness and self-appreciation expand within you. Think of it as replenishing yourself emotionally, ensuring you operate from a place of gratitude and abundance. Remember, you are just as deserving of your own love, care, and gratitude as anyone else.

Let your cup overflow with self-gratitude, end your day with a heart full of gratitude, and maintain that beaming smile.

Conclusion

When you arise in the morning, think of what a privilege it is to be alive, to think, to enjoy, to love. –Marcus Aurelius

The art of gratitude is a daily practice. Yes, whether it be rain or snow, through thick or thin, gratitude should form an integral part of your daily life, unfailingly.

Sure, when the going gets tough, practicing gratitude can be rather challenging. However, it's during these curveball moments that you need to tap into this superpower even more. When you are having a disagreement with your partner, it's the perfect time to reflect on something you cherish about them. Maybe, they handled the morning rush, took the kids to school, took out the trash, or brought you a loving cup of coffee. Or perhaps, something at work snagged your day. Pause and be grateful for the job you hold—a privilege many people don't have. Relish in all the resources it provides. Be grateful for the money you earn that enables you to afford the things you need and want. If your four-legged, furry friend erred on the rug, keep your cool and appreciate the unconditional love and comfort they provide you.

Perhaps, you find yourself stuck in traffic, soaking in the details around you. Is there a pet in the car ahead, peering out with trusting eyes? Allow the moment to fill your heart with the warmth and joy of gratitude. What about the mom strolling along, hand-in-hand with her little one? Bask in the gratitude of love. And if you find yourself driving alongside a learner driver, remember the early days when you embarked on that same journey filled with adventure, nerves, and excitement. Instead of focusing on what's wrong, hunt for the positives in any situation. You can consciously change frustration into gratitude by merely shifting your perspective. By consciously adjusting your perspective, you can transform frustration into gratitude. Gratitude grants you the power to step out of a scarcity mindset and straight into a more positive, abundance mindset.

As you can see, there is always something to be grateful for every single day. You just have to pay attention; life is in the details. Embrace the gifts that surround you, irrespective of how big or small they are. Every little blessing counts; they all add up, contributing to a greater whole of pure fulfillment. You hold the power to choose when and how to weave the art of gratitude into your daily life. Each day is a new day, and you will always have new things to celebrate with the abundance of life that surrounds you. What are the things you want to celebrate and be grateful for every day? Following the 14 steps throughout the book has undoubtedly unlocked more joy and fulfillment within you. Your job is to keep it up, keeping your gratitude flame burning. If you are feeling stressed, let gratitude be your anchor. If your inner critic gets too loud, silence it with a wholesome dose of self-gratitude. And when your emotions are running high, ground yourself in a moment of gratitude.

Gratitude is your wise mentor, reminding you that though things will not always go your way, irrespective of what you are going through, there's always a positive to be drawn from it. Gratitude is the lens that allows you to see the world from a perspective of possibilities and abundance. Always keep in mind that your life is woven from the threads of the relationships you foster and the experiences you have. These two fundamental aspects are what you draw from, enabling you to reveal the rich tapestry of gratitude.

Gratitude is the magical elixir that opens the doors to whole new worlds. It's a powerful force that forges strong relationships, improves our physical and mental well-being, tames aggression, amplifies empathy, fortifies resilience, and boosts self-esteem. These benefits are merely the tip of the iceberg when it comes to gratitude. You have dipped your toes into the waters of gratitude and can feel the positive effects already taking root in your life. Think of it as a gentle force that amplifies your positive experiences, adding significant value to each day. It's a gift that keeps on giving. I am sure at this point you don't need any further convincing of the incredible impact of gratitude.

In addition to using gratitude as a powerful tool for enhancing emotional regulation during challenging times, it's pivotal to uphold this practice as a daily ritual. Thus, be sure to treasure every step of this wonderful journey because you are at the beginning of an incredible chapter in your life as you unlock the power of gratitude. Embrace it with an open mind.

Kick off every day with your heart filled with gratitude, and sprinkle it throughout the minutes and hours. Also, don't forget to wrap your day up in the warm embrace of yet another moment of gratitude.

Remember to smile! Smile as much as you can! It's contagious, and you'll find it spreading far and wide!

References

Ali, A. (2022, March 28). *The Importance of Mental Peace | Physical health.* Medium. https://medium.com/@aamnaameerali/the-importance-of-mental-peace-physical-health-afd5413e4ce6

Appreciation Of Nature Quotes (22 quotes). (2023). Www.goodreads.com. https://www.goodreads.com/quotes/tag/appreciat ion-of-nature

Bradley, J. (2020, December 15). *Children teaching adults about joy, fun, gratitude and approaching each moment with a clean slate.* Learnful with Jo Bradley. https://www.learnful.co.uk/2020/12/15/children-teaching-adults-mindfulness-2/

Caprino, K. (2014, June 2). *9 Core Behaviors Of People Who Positively Impact The World.* Forbes. https://www.forbes.com/sites/kathycaprino/2014 /06/02/9-core-behaviors-of-people-who-positively-impact-the-world/?sh=249c69296b41

Cassetty, S. (2021, August 24). *How to accept your body, even if you don't love every inch of it.* TODAY.com. https://www.today.com/health/7-ways-learn-accept-appreciate-your-body-today-t228957

David. (2022, April 12). *How To Appreciate What You Have: 13 Tips.* Handwrytten. https://www.handwrytten.com/resources/how-to-appreciate-what-you-have/

8 Simple Ways to Appreciate Your Body Every Day. (2022, July 1). infrontadmin. *Truesport.org.* https://truesport.org/body-image/8-ways-appreciate-your-body/

Field, B. (2022, August 8). *The Importance of Family Love.* Verywell Mind. https://www.verywellmind.com/family-love-how-to-create-it-and-sustain-it-5193643#:~:text=A%20family

Ghekiere, E. (2018, April 17). *40 Ways to Practice Gratitude for Yourself and Others.* Page Flutter. https://pageflutter.com/40-ways-to-practice-gratitude/

Gratitude and Self-Love. (n.d.). Https://Www.borntobeworthless.com/. https://www.borntobeworthless.com/gratitude-self-love/

Gratitude: Fun Facts and App Recommendations. (n.d.). anchor_admin. *Three Rivers Therapy.* https://www.3riverstherapy.com/gratitude-journals/

Haden, J. (2014, September 12). *40 Inspiring Motivational Quotes About Gratitude.* Inc.com. https://www.inc.com/jeff-haden/40-inspiring-motivational-quotes-about-gratitude.html

Harmony. (2018, May 8). *23 Ways To Instil Appreciation For Nature And The Environment in Your Child.* Harmony Learning. https://harmonylearning.com.au/23-ways-to-instil-appreciation-for-nature-and-the-environment-in-your-child/

Horsley, G. (2021, November 23). *Council Post: Three Ways To Move Forward With Gratitude After Loss.* Forbes. https://www.forbes.com/sites/forbesnonprofitcouncil/2021/11/23/three-ways-to-move-forward-with-gratitude-after-loss/?sh=2020e289601b

How to Appreciate What You Have and Stop Comparing Yourself to Others. (2022). Happify.com. https://www.happify.com/hd/how-to-appreciate-what-you-have/

How to Enjoy Work. (2022, December 20). Indeed Editorial Team. *Indeed Career Guide.* https://www.indeed.com/career-advice/career-development/how-to-enjoy-work

How to Take Effective Breaks (and be more productive). (2023). Www.deprocrastination.co. https://www.deprocrastination.co/blog/how-to-take-effective-breaks-and-be-more-productive

Howells, D. K. (2017, February 15). *Gratitude to Self.* Grateful.org. https://grateful.org/grateful-living/gratitude-to-self/

If you want to feel more resilient, thank a stranger. (2022, November 20) Gratitude Gravy. LA Rockstar Creative.

https://www.larockstarcreative.com/blog/give-thanks-to-a-stranger

Johnson, S. (2022, August 10). *What Is Self-Gratitude and How Can You Practice It? | Cake Blog.* Www.joincake.com. https://www.joincake.com/blog/self-gratitude/#h_480517264216456340228411

Kraft, R. N. (2021, May 7). *10 Benefits of Making Lists | Psychology Today.* Www.psychologytoday.com. https://www.psychologytoday.com/us/blog/defining-memories/202105/10-benefits-making-lists

Lamothe , C. (2019, April 24). *How to Be a Better Person to Others and Yourself.* Healthline. https://www.healthline.com/health/how-to-be-a-better-person

Lauren. (2015, November 5). *71 Ways to Show Gratitude to Family, Friends, and Strangers.* Oh, Honestly! https://ohhonestly.net/71-ways-to-show-gratitude-to-family-friends-and-strangers/

Markman, A. (2016, August 2). *This Is the Secret to Getting Anything Done | Psychology Today.* Www.psychologytoday.com. https://www.psychologytoday.com/us/blog/ulterior-motives/201608/is-the-secret-getting-anything-done

Milletto, B. (2019, July 5). *Gratitude Turns What We Have Into Enough.* Thrive Global. https://community.thriveglobal.com/gratitude-turns-what-we-have-into-enough/

Munshi, D. (2022, October 11). *How to Practice Gratitude & Improve Your Family's Mental Health.* HealthyChildren.org. https://www.healthychildren.org/English/healthy-living/emotional-wellness/Building-Resilience/Pages/how-to-practice-gratitude.aspx#:~:text=Focus%20on%20what%20went%20%22right

Nahoul, B. (2023). *The Facts of Gratitude: The Numerous Physical and Mental Health Benefits of Gratitude Practice.* https://experiencecle.com/the-facts-of-gratitude-the-numerous-physical-and-mental-health-benefits-of-gratitude-practice/

Nayak, A. (2020, August 17). *You Should Absolutely Take a Break Right Now—And Here's the Best Way to Do It.* Architectural Digest. https://www.architecturaldigest.com/story/take-a-break-mental-health-screen-time#:~:text=%E2%80%9CTaking%20breaks%20allows%20your%20brain

Phil. (2019, November 29). *Finding Gratitude for What Your Body Can Do.* Step & Spine. https://stepandspine.urpt.com/blog/finding-gratitude-for-what-your-body-can-do/

Plato Quote: "A grateful mind is a great mind which eventually attracts to itself great things." (2023). Quotefancy.com. https://quotefancy.com/quote/888574/Plato-A-grateful-mind-is-a-great-mind-which-eventually-attracts-to-itself-great-things

Raypole, C. (2020, April 27). *Can You Ever Really Forgive Someone?* Healthline. https://www.healthline.com/health/how-to-forgive#takeaway

Reasons It's Important To Honor Your Lost Loved One. (2022, June 14). Crockett County Times. https://crockettcountytimes.com/reasons-its-important-to-honor-your-lost-loved-one/

Reid, S. (2023, February 28). *Gratitude: The Benefits and How to Practice It - HelpGuide.org.* Https://Www.helpguide.org. https://www.helpguide.org/articles/mental-health/gratitude.htm

Robbins, M. (2022, November 29). *Why Taking Breaks Is So Important.* Https://Mike-Robbins.com/. https://mike-robbins.com/why-taking-breaks-is-so-important/

The Role of Reminders in Achieving Goals - a Psychological Perspective. (2023, January 25). ReminderCall. *A Rectangle Health Company.* https://www.remindercall.com/resources/role-of-reminders-in-achieving-goals/

Rose, R. (2023, February 25). *Questions To Ask Yourself After Failure.* Your Perfect Dreams.

https://www.yourperfectdreams.com/questions-to-ask-yourself-after-failure/

Shenck, Laura. (2011, October 3). *The Importance of How You Think About Mistakes - Mindfulness Muse*. Www.mindfulnessmuse.com. https://www.mindfulnessmuse.com/psychology-research/the-importance-of-how-you-think-about-mistakes

Tanguay, J. (2023, August 31). *20 Creative Ways to Honor a Loved One After They Died | Cake Blog*. Www.joincake.com. https://www.joincake.com/blog/creative-ways-to-honor-someone/

10 Reasons We Should Celebrate Our Planet. (2017, October 22). THE ENVIRONMENTOR. https://blog.tentree.com/10-reasons-we-should-celebrate-our-planet/

Top 25 Appreciation in Relationships Quotes. (n.d.). A-Z Quotes. Retrieved October 24, 2023, from https://www.azquotes.com/quotes/topics/appreciation-in-relationships.html

Weir, K. (2020). Nurtured by nature. *American Psychological Association*, *51*(3). https://www.apa.org/monitor/2020/04/nurtured-nature

"When I started counting my blessings, my whole life turned around." —*Willie Nelson*. (2023). The Foundation for a Better Life. https://www.passiton.com/inspirational-

quotes/4614-when-i-started-counting-my-blessings-my-whole

Why It's Important That We Value Nature. (n.d.). WWF. https://www.wwf.org.uk/what-we-do/valuing-nature#:~:text=Our%20forests%2C%20rivers%2C%20oceans%20and

Wooll, M. (2022a, September 13). *Gratitude at Work: Don't Hate, Appreciate!* Www.betterup.com. https://www.betterup.com/blog/gratitude-at-work

Wooll, M. (2022b, January 27). *Learn From Your Mistakes: Master This Art to Achieve More.* Www.betterup.com. https://www.betterup.com/blog/learning-from-your-mistakes

Image References

Be, H. (2016). [Image]. In *Unsplash.* https://unsplash.com/photos/orange-flowers-IicyiaPYGGI

Becker, G. (2017). [Image]. In *Pexels.* https://www.pexels.com/photo/1-1-3-text-on-black-chalkboard-374918/

Dumlao, N. (2020). [Image]. In *Unsplash.* https://unsplash.com/photos/person-holding-white-and-black-i-love-you-print-card-fs_l0Xqlc90

Fotios, L. (2019). [Image]. In *Pexels*. https://www.pexels.com/photo/three-pairs-of-shoes-1909014/

Hazelwood, S. (2019). [Image]. In *Pexels*. https://www.pexels.com/photo/assorted-photos-on-table-1989747/

Hedger, C. (2017). Thank You wooden cubes [Image]. In *Unsplash*. https://unsplash.com/photos/thank-you-on-wooden-blocks-t48eHCSCnds

Lastovich, T. (2017). [Image]. In *Pexels*. https://www.pexels.com/photo/black-iphone-7-on-brown-table-699122/

Long, R. (2021). A child's hands imprint showing their love [Image]. In *Unsplash*. https://unsplash.com/photos/3-brown-hand-with-white-background-89bQBucvJdw

Merakist. (2019). Work in Colorful Alphabets [Image]. In *Unsplash*. https://unsplash.com/photos/work-freestanding-letters-zFd9Zvs0yN8

Parera, M. (2020). [Image]. In *Unsplash*. https://unsplash.com/photos/blue-and-white-abstract-painting-gridDcZPsK8

Peterson-Hall, R. (2019). @thevibrantmachine holding candle in october [Image]. In *Unsplash*. https://unsplash.com/photos/lighted-candles-aN-zGYlxiCI

poan, A. (2020). [Image]. In *Pexels*. https://www.pexels.com/photo/opened-notebook-with-pencil-and-paintbrush-5797912/

Robbins, B. (2020). [Image]. In *Unsplash*. https://unsplash.com/photos/silver-framed-eyeglasses-on-yellow-surface-S20PlUJRviI

Sikkema, K. (2017). Ideas waiting to be had [Image]. In *Unsplash*. https://unsplash.com/photos/six-white-sticky-notes--1_RZL8BGBM

Sikkema, K. (2020). man and woman holding a heart together [Image]. In *Unsplash*. https://unsplash.com/photos/two-person-holding-papercut-heart-4le7k9XVYjE

Цветановић, A. (2018). [Image]. In *Pexels*. https://www.pexels.com/photo/close-up-photo-of-person-holding-red-apple-1451649/

Yasser, K. (2017). [Image]. In *Unsplash*. https://unsplash.com/photos/heart-drawn-on-sand-during-daytime-FHT0KEOwtyg

Made in United States
Troutdale, OR
12/05/2023